God, Please WAKE UP MY ADAM!
He Is in a Coma!

BY DR. VERYL HOWARD

Copyright © 2026 Dr. Veryl Howard

All rights reserved.

No part of this publication may be reproduced, distributed, or transmitted in any form or by any means, including photocopying, recording, or other electronic or mechanical methods, without the prior written permission of the publisher, except in the case of brief quotations embodied in critical reviews and certain other non-commercial uses permitted by copyright law.

ISBN: 979-8-218-87572-5

Edit and Layout by Shonell Bacon
Publishing Coach: Telishia Berry

Dedication

My God, who has healed me through and through, during every bad relationship and every step I take in life.

The men who meant loss for me and gain for themselves. Because of you and God's healing, I had the strength to put pen to paper.

Elder Tara Hughes, Telishia Berry, and Anna Stephenson, who created a safe space for me to unleash my emotions. You truly toughed it out with me.

Aunt Audrey Hinton, Cynthia Howard, Kim Howard and Uncle Alvin Hinton, I dedicate this book to you all, too, because you have been there for me through the hurts and pains of relationships.

Table of Contents

	Foreword by Anna Stephenson	i
	Foreword by Telishia Berry	iii
	Preface	v
	Acknowledgments	vii
Ch. 1	The "What Is Wrong with Me?" Syndrome	1
Ch. 2	The Settling Mentality	4
Ch. 3	The "What If..." Dilemma	9
Ch. 4	Your Type	12
Ch. 5	Are You Dressed for the Meeting?	14
Ch. 6	The Games Men Play Today	16
Ch. 7	The Narcissist	19
Ch. 8	The "I Can't Function Without Him" Syndrome	21
Ch. 9	The Snake, You're Being Watched	24
Ch. 10	Avoid These Men at All Costs!	27
Ch. 11	Why Does He Still Call You?	35
Ch. 12	Women, What Happens When the Right Man Shows Up?	39
Ch. 13	Are You Authentically You?	41
Ch. 14	When a Man Loves You and Treats You Right	44
Ch. 15	It Is Not a Competition Between You and Your Adam	46
Ch. 16	A Momma's Boy Versus a Mother's Love	48
Ch. 17	Take Off That Other Lady's Clothes	52

Ch. 18	God, My Body Is Changing, Please Send My Adam!	55
Ch. 19	Are You Prepared for Your Adam Like Esther?	62
Ch. 20	Do You Know Who You Are?	66
Ch. 21	Get Your Dignity Back!	69
	About Apostle Dr. Veryl Howard	73
	Dr. Veryl Howard & Family, Her Love	77

Foreword
By Anna Stephenson

When I started reading *God Please Wake Up My Adam He Is in a Coma!*, I couldn't stop until I finished it. The reason this book will bless many people is threefold.

Number #1: The revelation that's within this book is powerful. There is a great need in the church and the world today for revelation about who we really are and the things we tolerate in our lives.

Number #2: The message is built on *experience*, and people need to hear it. It is always better to take advice from somebody who has walked the road they are talking about.

Number #3: The transparency is appreciated because the reader will not feel like they are alone. Most single women will identify with the experiences that you share, and I'm sure a lot of single men will realize their true identity when they read about the different categories they fit in.

I'm honored to endorse this book because we all have a story to tell, but not all of us are brave enough to tell it. In this book, Apostle Dr. Veryl Howard gives a voice to the single ladies who know that they deserve better but don't know how to articulate it.

God, Please Wake Up My Adam He Is in a Coma! has stepped into a Kairos moment. A Kairos moment is a Greek term that signifies a special opportune time. I believe it's time for this book to come forward.

A Kairos moment is also a divinely appointed moment of significance; it's a turning point in your life. This book will be a turning point for everyone who embraces it.

Apostle Dr. Veryl Howard is not only a covenant friend but a leader that I have looked up to from the first time God allowed our Kingdom connection. She understands her assignment from God and walks in an anointing that's unique and powerful.

Anna Stephenson
Radio Host of *Spiritual Downloads*
Miami, Fl
Published Author

Foreword
By Telishia Berry

As a single, divorced woman who has lived through love, loss, disappointment, and renewal, I approached *God, Please Wake Up My Adam! He Is in a Coma!* with both honesty and vulnerability. Reading this book felt like sitting across from a sister who understands the pieces of my story that were too heavy to voice out loud. Dr. Veryl Howard writes with the courage, clarity, and compassion that many of us have longed to hear. Her words reach into the quiet places of the heart where hope and heartbreak often sit side by side.

This book is powerful because it speaks directly to the woman who has tried, trusted, forgiven, started over, and is still believing that God has not forgotten her. Dr. Veryl tackles the questions many divorced and single women wrestle with: How did I get here? Why did love fail me? Is real love still possible? What do I do when I am tired of starting again? She addresses these questions with biblical truth, raw transparency, and a refreshing boldness that reminds us of our worth.

Her stories echo the experiences of women who have loved deeply, been wounded deeply, and still desire a God-appointed love that brings peace and partnership rather than confusion and pain. She gives voice to the exhaustion of waiting, the temptation to settle, the frustration of counterfeits, and the longing to be truly seen. She also reminds us that even after divorce, disappointment, or delay, God still restores and redirects with purpose.

This book challenges us to reclaim our dignity, heal emotionally, rise spiritually, and prepare ourselves with intention rather than fear. It teaches us that waiting is not weakness and singleness after divorce is not failure. It is an opportunity for God to strengthen what was broken and awaken what is still possible.

For every woman who has been divorced and wondered if love would ever find her again…

For every woman who has been single longer than she expected…

For every woman who still believes that God can rewrite a story at any age or stage…

This book is for us.

May these pages remind you that God still sees you, values you, and is shaping you for a love that aligns with destiny. He has not forgotten you. Your Adam will wake up, and when he does, he will recognize the woman God has refined for such a time as this.

Telishia Berry
Publishing Coach and Author

Preface

After years and years of crying out to the Lord about my mate, I decided to write this book. Many people prophesied over me repeatedly and said my husband was coming. They even tried to describe him. I have now passed many seasons and no man, so I questioned whether or not they were true prophets. Did they lie to me? Were they in their flesh? Or was it just not the right timing? So, God, when is it? That is a real question many single women like myself ask. We wait year after year as we try to hold on to our youthful bodies and wrinkle free faces. We panic when we see strands of gray hair or lines on our face. We ask ourselves who would want us now past what folks call a ripe ole age. Well, we just keep hope alive, believing if God said it, he will get it done on his time.

Like many women, I have attended several weddings wondering when will I be found. I have experienced many holidays, family events, movie trips, and festivities alone. Some of them I would even avoid because it was about the family unit and not the single woman stage. I would always end up going home alone having to cheer myself up. I would even go to the shopping mall to buy something and not be alone. Basically, I have been the only single person in the place, and I am flat out over it.

Many of my friends can't identify with where I am at this juncture in life. They are on grown children going to college or grandchildren. Many want out of their marriages, or they feel stuck. Some are even on marriage number three while others are living a life of a lie. They tell me it is not all it's cracked up to be and enjoy being single. Well, that is not encouraging because I look forward to the unity and someone having my back. I look forward to my natural and spiritual covering from my man. Two can accomplish more together when on the same page then one. I have had great success as a single woman, but I have enough sense to know when me and my man are on the same page, the sky is the limit! I am his rib walking around waiting to fit into the purpose God has given him for both of us together.

Therefore, like many other women, I have wondered if it is ever going to happen for me. I did not sign up to be a eunuch or nun. I have real desires, needs, and wants to be loved, too. I am not trying to spread myself thin and taint myself with spiritual baggage. So, I am sure I speak on behalf of several beautiful, talented, smart women who have it going on, but yet they are still single. While many are working on their second or third marriage, we are still waiting for number one.

I *had* to write this book in hopes of encouraging others and letting them know they are not alone. So, if that is your story, too, I am sure you will be able to identify with these chapters. If you are a man and still sleeping, this book may wake you up so you can claim your rib.

Acknowledgments

This book was inspired by the unfortunate trials of dating, so to the men who helped give me these testimonies, thank you to every man who ever had ill intentions with me and acted on it. You were instrumental in draining, stripping, and disrespecting me so God could build me up. Thank you because my unfortunate relationships with the wrong Adam showed me God's true love and who I really was as a woman of God. You were instrumental in my growth as a woman who loves the Lord. The Bible says, in Romans 8:28 KJV, that "28 And we know that all things work together for good to them that love God, to them who are the called according to his purpose."

Thank you is not strong enough to acknowledge my God. God for pulling me through every circumstance that was not conducive to my well-being. If it was not for God constantly healing me, I would not have been able to continue to thrive. It was because of God's love for me I was able to endure and overcome many hurts and disappointments. His love showed me how to forgive and love again. God, I thank you above all for being my healer.

Thank you to all my true girlfriends who prayed with or talked me through my heartaches after a bad relationship. Tamera Fair, what can I say? You keep it real by keeping me grounded and not allowing me to let any man discredit me or use me while trying to keep me down. I appreciate you talking me back into reality. Jokia Williams, thanks for the no nonsense talks of encouragement. You and Lucinda Moore have kept it one hundred with me and I appreciate all your prayers. Benjamin, you are blunt and tell it like it is. Thank you for that.

Thank you to my family the Howards for letting me camp out when I had rough tear-jerking lonely moments. Especially my nieces and nephews Benton, Bryant aka Roo, Chloe Bene', Blaire, and Brian Jr. who always knew how to lift auntie's spirit. Little did they know depression had gripped me at times because I was tired of being alone. Their hugs made a difference in many moments where I just wanted to give up. They have loved me when I felt unloved. Auntie loves you, and you have been a gift from God to me. Brielle, you hanging out with Auntie just makes my day.

To my brothers Brian Howard and Ben Ben aka Bennie Howard, who will not give me any advice, I appreciate you protecting your sister from the wolves. I know one day Brian, I will come to you with the right one and you all are going to have to get to know him. So, hang in their brothers, I know you want your sister blessed and it's coming. I trust in God!

Thank you to my aunt Audrey and uncle Alvin who had to tag team when I lost my mother. Their advice while living with them really helped me through some dark moments. They were there when no man was there to console me about my mom's death though I was dating one at the time.

Pastor Deitrick Haddon, Ashford Sanders, Tri Cray Astwood, Pastor Guy Reeves and Apostle Buie, you all have been instrumental in helping me out with this man thang. It's nothing like hearing it from real brothers in Christ. I know you all want me happy for real, so I appreciate your candid advice.

Thank you to Prophetess Anna Stephenson and Telishia Berry who wrote my forewords. They have been confidants over the years as we all wait for our mates. Thank you to my graphic designer Hope Stilth who gets me. Thank you to Elder Tara and her husband Nate aka Joe who have had to pray me through some rough relationship situations. They have warred with me in the spirit against demons that wanted to take me out in dangerous relationships. Thank you, Pastor Sherry Grant, who counseled me when I was about to lose my mind over a man who wanted to marry me and disappeared after he could not manipulate and use me. He just happened to be a pastor.

Thank you to my heavenly mom who pushed me to write at such a young age. Rest in heaven, Mom. Your daughter misses you, but you taught me how to press on regardless. You were a beautiful example of strength in a woman. Thank you to my heavenly dad who taught me though I did not listen to leave some of the knuckle heads alone even at a young age. He also taught me and my friend Patria about diseases way before they were an epidemic, and he warned us not to get trapped by them. He knew it was a trick to keep us from our Adam. May they both rest in peace.

Thank you to all who read my book and found some tool they could use to be better equipped for the time when their Adam finds them.

Chapter One

THE "WHAT IS WRONG WITH ME?" SYNDROME

If you have lived past your so-called married years according to society, I am sure you have asked this question before. You have probably wondered: am I too fat, too short, too dark, too light, too smart, not smart enough, too successful, too skinny or questioned any imperfections you may have. You ask these questions because you see others who have had children, been married, and in some cases, been ready for a divorce. They question you as to why you want to rush into marriage. Well, being over forty, fifty, or even sixty in some cases is not rushing. Go figure. But you question yourself. I call it a syndrome because you began to doubt you and what you have to offer. You can be fine as grape wine, educated with a bomb figure, successful, and have great credit yet still be single. So, you wondered, "What is wrong with me?" You forgot you meant something to the Lord and others who value you. Because you are wrapped up in this syndrome regardless of your success, you doubt you. Been there, done that, and I can identify. Somebody say I am tired of this mindset!

Let's look at this syndrome thang a little closer. According to Webster, a syndrome is defined as a group of signs and symptoms that occur together and characterize a particular abnormality or condition or secondly a set of concurrent things (such as emotions or actions) that usually form an identifiable pattern. So, in other words, you start believing there is some abnormality in you or some insufficiency in you because you are still single. You rotate periodically in a pattern, feeling less than powerful because your emotions get the best of you. Even after you snap back around, a new holiday can trigger these feelings again, thus exhibiting the pattern. FYI, it does not matter how bad you are or how great your job, bank account, or credit is, you can still have this syndrome. The sad part is your friends who are married can't really identify with your pain though they try. At the end of the day, they go back to their man.

So, what do you do? Well, I have had my ups and downs. I have eaten a pint of ice cream and stopped caring, and I have also tried to better me. None the less, I am still single. I had to knock sense into my head and decree that single or not, I will be the best I can be. That means figure, credit, wisdom, appearance, business, and more. I just got to a point where I was no longer going to just let me go!

You married women have your man as a check and balance. Your man will say, *Baby, you getting thick... Baby, I like your hair this (or that) way...* or *Bae, I got your back.* Married women are constantly watched by her husband. Trust me, if she slips too much, he is looking at someone else. But single people don't have that iron sharpening iron as the Bible says, so they must check themselves. Trust me, that gets hard at times because while waiting, many may think, *Well I been keeping it together all this time, but I am still single. So again, what is wrong with me? I am a great catch. How did my friend April get so blessed, and she does not have half as much going for herself as I do?* Well, the Bible says, "Compare yourself to no one." 2 Corinthians 10:12-16 KJV furthers this thought with

> 12 For we dare not make ourselves of the number, or compare ourselves with some that commend themselves: but they measuring themselves by themselves, and comparing themselves among themselves, are not wise. 13 But we will not boast of things without our measure, but according to the measure of the rule which God hath distributed to us, a measure to reach even unto you.

How dare me anyhow. She has her man!

So, the cycle of this syndrome continues as time passes bye. HELP! I was put on this earth to be fruitful and multiply. I was purposed by God to procreate! But my womb is tired though kept and cleansed. I am past birthing years in the natural, so what was God talking about? I feel humiliated like Hannah in the Bible who was barren and mocked. Does God want to do me like Sarah and Hannah in the Bible? Does he want to open up my womb? Do I even have the stamina for all of that at this age? Naw, multiply does not just mean your natural womb. Be fruitful with your purpose and assignment. I am trying but keeping it real, it gets hard.

God, free me from this syndrome! Free me like you did Sarah and Hannah!

Chapter Two

THE SETTLING MENTALITY

Ok, ladies, I know you been there. You got tired of sitting at home alone, so you decided to go out with someone you know you are not attracted to in any capacity. You don't even like the man, but you're tired of waiting. He even had the audacity to trip, and he is clueless he is not your type. You were giving him a chance, but he is acting like he has it all together like a Casanova. I've been there, settling with a man who still wanted to play games at his ripe age. Now, I am not going to settle but have the best God has for me when he comes. I was minimizing me by accepting what came my way to keep from being lonely. Not anymore. Those situations were "How dare you?" moments. They were also a waste of my time.

Many women marry the wrong one because they are exhausted from waiting. They rather learn to love that man and be unequally yoked than be alone. I get it! Just not for me. I tried but could not even take the ring. Don't do it, it's a trap! You lower your standards and end up unhappy because the spark and connection were never there.

You try to manipulate a situation because you were tired of being alone. Maybe he is a smoker, and you hate smoke, but you think, *Well a little smoke will be ok.* Maybe he swings both ways, and you are willing to turn the cheek to be with a man. Or maybe you are a devout believer in Christ, but he is not. You just have nothing in common with the man but some good sex. I serve you notice It takes more than sex to keep a marriage. Just maybe he has a drinking habit, and you think you can pray or rationalize it away. NOT! Why settle if you believe God?

Here is something from the Good Word of the Bible to help you understand your value. It's long, but so necessary, so take your time in reading. Genesis 2:1 states

> Thus, the heavens and the earth were completed in all their vast array. 2 By the seventh day God had finished the work he had been doing; so, on the seventh day he rested from all his work. 3 Then God blessed the seventh day and made it holy, because on it he rested from all the work of creating that he had done. Adam and Eve 4 This is the account of the heavens and the earth when they were created, when the Lord God made the earth and the heavens. 5 Now no shrub had yet appeared on the earth[a] and no plant had yet sprung up, for the Lord God had not sent rain on the earth and there was no one to work the ground, 6 but streams came up from the earth and watered the whole surface of the ground. 7 Then the Lord God formed a man from the dust of the ground and breathed into his nostrils the breath of life, and the man became a living being. 8 Now the Lord God had planted a garden in the east, in Eden; and there he put the man he had formed. 9 The Lord God made all kinds of trees grow out of the ground—trees that were

pleasing to the eye and good for food. In the middle of the garden were the tree of life and the tree of the knowledge of good and evil.

10 A river watering the garden flowed from Eden; from there it was separated into four headwaters. 11 The name of the first is the Pishon; it winds through the entire land of Havilah, where there is gold. 12 (The gold of that land is good; aromatic resin[d] and onyx are also there.) 13 The name of the second river is the Gihon; it winds through the entire land of Cush. 14 The name of the third river is the Tigris; it runs along the east side of Ashur. And the fourth river is the Euphrates. 15 The Lord God took the man and put him in the Garden of Eden to work it and take care of it. 16 And the Lord God commanded the man, "You are free to eat from any tree in the garden; 17 but you must not eat from the tree of the knowledge of good and evil, for when you eat from it you will certainly die.

Now, pay attention to this next passage:

18 The Lord God said, *"It is not good for the man to be alone. I will make a helper suitable for him."* **That's you, ladies!** 19 Now the Lord God had formed out of the ground all the wild animals and all the birds in the sky. He brought them to the man to see what he would name them; and whatever the man called each living creature, that was its name. 20 So the man gave names to all the livestock, the birds in the sky and all the wild animals.

Wow, before you, man had a responsibility to name all the animals—all by himself. So, he was successful and obedient but still alone. God does the inevitable out of his compassion to see us loved with a companion as well. He gives man a helpmate. You are somebody's helpmate that needs to be found.

But for Adam, no suitable helper was found.

21 So the Lord God caused the man to fall into a deep sleep; and while he was sleeping, he took one of the man's ribs and then closed up the place with flesh. 22 *Then the Lord God made a woman from the rib he had taken out of the man, and he brought her to the man.*

Ok, I have been made already, like you, from my man's rib. So now, it's time for my man to wake up and describe who I am to him!!!

23 The man [Adam] said, *"This is now bone of my bones and flesh of my flesh; she shall be called 'woman,' for she was taken out of man.*

Adam knows where his woman came from. He named her, and she is now a part of him multiplied. She is his flesh that he needs to cherish. That is why man leaves his father and mother and is united to his wife for them to become one flesh (Genesis 2:24).

Hum, direction is given here. Once they cleave, the woman now has his identity as **one**, but her own separate one, too.

The woman is described as the female of the human species, created by God as distinct from, but equal to, man. Biblical texts emphasize women's unique roles as life-givers, helpers, and bearers of God's image, while also highlighting their capacity for wisdom, strength, and faith. Her role is a part for man's purpose. My, my, my, where is my oneness though we are two?

Your man may be sleep like mine, and it is time for him to wake up! I was formed, now I must do what I was called to do. Maybe your man is awoke but he does not recognize who you are. He needs some revelation. Like many women, men settle, too. Big booty, tight dress, and a thirsty woman will get them every time. Some are just willing to be seen and do what you will not do. Adam lets flesh override purpose and does not see you. Pray that your man is not memorized by the deceptive lurking spirit of today. Pray you can be seen for who you are as his helper. I pray the veil or scales comes off, so we all can be seen by our man who is trying to find us.

Chapter Three

THE "WHAT IF..." DILEMMA

Have you ever gone back over your life and tried to recap what you thought you missed out on? You played the same scenario over and over in your head wondering what you did wrong. You start blaming yourself because maybe you thought you missed it. Well snap out of it! The time has passed. Think about the new and prepare for that regardless of the date. Don't let your past disrupt your future. Maybe he married the wrong one, and his life was one of misery. You knew it was supposed to be you. You were on your way to the altar. Ok in tough terms, so what? God has better. You have endured for the prize.

Maybe you made the wrong choice and turned away the good guy, and then the man you were going to marry turned out to be a creep. Well, God has some more good guys out here, I just don't know where, or I would have one. But I am trusting him anyhow. Maybe you were mentally not in a space for marriage, but he was. He did not decide to wait, and now you see him being successful.

Don't get clipped up by that; you don't know the inside story. Your man coming—just get prepared.

Listen, ladies, keep thriving, keep building, keep your head up, and by all means, keep believing that you have purpose. You not here to be miserable in your singleness. You have value single or not. Don't let the lack of a man define your preciousness. You are still the apple of God's eyes, and he will love you through it all. I know it's not easy because I am a living witness. When I get down and depressed, I have to encourage myself. I have to remind myself I am a great woman of God. I have to have pep talks with myself. My married friends don't know how to encourage me, so it's me and God. I try to avoid bitter women who are always in that doubting, sorrowful stage because I do not want to get my spirits down. So, I work, plan, build, create, multiply and make myself more valuable.

One very successful man told me he would never marry a woman who did not have her own house at our age. Another told me he is not marrying any woman with less than a seven hundred credit score because it speaks volumes as to how she is living at this older age. So that was the criteria for him because so many women were approaching him with a come-up spirit. God created us equally. I am not looking for a come up. I am looking for my soul mate, a man who will love and appreciate me and know I am a gift from God. I want my man, and I don't mind submitting to him as it states in the Bible. Check out Ephesians 5:22:

> Wives, submit yourselves to your own husbands as you do to the Lord. 23 For the husband is the head of the wife as Christ is the head of the church, his body, of which he is the Savior. 24 Now as the church

submits to Christ, so also wives should submit to their husbands in everything.

But I come with the goods myself. I come as an asset not a liability. Ladies, be the asset he needs. You are the helper not the helpless!

Chapter Four

YOUR TYPE

Ladies, if you are like me, your type has evolved. What you liked in your 20s or 30s is not the same. You have matured and been through some things. You know what you can tolerate and what you can't. You should have a better idea of your identity by now. You should be more comfortable with you and your assignment while walking this earth. So, we must be careful of wanting that same type of dude that caused us drama in our younger years. We sometimes fall for the same tricks over and over—with different men. We like them tall, light, and fine or tall, chiseled, dark, and beefed up. But what does God have for us? Obviously, he knows and we don't because we're still single.

Sometimes, our appetite trips us up, and we fall back in the same situation. I stepped out my normal type and my non type thought they were all of that. But I had stepped into the same characteristics my bad relationships had. I stepped into a situation with a man with the same demeanor though he looked different. It was a familiar spirit to me. I needed an appetite adjustment from the type of character I liked. I realized I was attracting the same type of jerks, so something had to change. It was me and my taste buds.

So, I had to ask God, "What is my appetite? What matches the man you pulled me from?" I knew it was one that I would like because God developed my taste buds. How do I prepare for the man with this appetite? Maybe my appetite is way bigger than I thought, and I have to adjust my mindset. Whoever my other half is, this new appetite must be for him, the husband God selected. I am staying prepared not to miss him. I have even checked my attitude, making sure I am more meek and subtle. Over the years, my patience was running short, but I have checked it. I am not to be taken advantage of, but I approach matters differently now that I have a new appetite.

Yes, I want to be attracted to my future husband, but I don't want him to misappropriate me. I want to find my man sexy, but I don't want him to value me with only that. I want my man to be successful, but I don't want him arrogant and rude. So, my appetite has changed. It's not all about the looks and the perfect buffed body anymore. Now, I don't want him fat and sloppy with no health consciousness. I am not going to be a hospice wife. I need my man to be health conscious naturally and spiritually. He has to bring more to the table and so do I, for we were created as equals.

Chapter Five

ARE YOU DRESSED FOR THE MEETING?

Back in the day, when my body was all of that, I dressed in exhibition mode. I knew my body could attract men and lure them in. I had no shame as I dressed half-naked and had clothes on so tight I could not breathe. I was on a mission. But what I did not realize was I was attracting a certain type of man that wanted all of that. I was younger, so what did I care? But did I bring any of that into my later years? We all want to look good. But believe it or not, our attire attracts certain types of men. There was even a study done where hairstyles attracted a certain caliber of man.

Shaved blonde hair, a bob, cornrows, and long hair all attracted different types of men. It was proven in a study. Now, I am not saying don't have your swag. I am just saying to be appropriate for whom you want to attract. Know the room. Don't be fifty but dressed like you thirty with everything hanging out at a business party. Many women these days have BBLs, and we all know men like big buttocks. But does the world have to see your panty creases? A certain class of men are not attracted to that. Men are visual, so it becomes more like a sexual desire versus a potential mate desire. So be dressed for the atmosphere. Be appropriate for your age. Now I like to keep myself in shape and youthful. I like spandex shorts, etc. because I work out a lot. But I have to know when and where. I want my mate to look at me and say she is wife material. I just try to be classy sexy.

I had to have a pep talk again with me. Because I used to love dressing to expose a lot of my body because of my figure. But that was a dumb gesture back in the day that became a habit for me. I had to break that habit. I had to find a balance between being well kept, sexy, classy, and holy. No man wants a woman that looks like everybody has touched her. In the church or out. So, I've been working on me because this is about my destiny and purpose with my mate. I am not going to let no hot pant shorts keep me from being found.

Chapter Six

THE GAMES MEN PLAY TODAY

When it comes to the games the men are playing these days. I am so out the loop. I feel so clueless. I am too old to try to figure out all these games. I am speaking of men over fifty who I would expect more from. I know the youngins must be on another level because what I have been dealing with is mind blowing. I feel like I almost have to date five men to get one decent one. The mind games are crazy.

I had my first encounters with the MIA man or the submarine man which I will explain in a second. Someone had to school me because I was dumbfounded. I also ran into the man looking for the hospice wife or nurse with a purse like my new friends Beverly and Marsi from Nevis said. Let's not even talk about LOVE BOMBMING. I thought what on earth? This is too much for dating.

Let's get back to the submarine man., I had never heard of this term until I saw it on Tik Tok. Listen me and this man had a wonderful time together on dates. We seemed to mesh and he met my requirements in a man. He was in ministry as I am in ministry. We had similar goals and both of us worldwide travelers. He even let me meet his child. He seemed to have liked me. I saw his house, hung out with him and his child and he disappeared on me. Who does that? I thought our meetings were great, but he vanished in thin air. Then a month later he resurfaced as if nothing was wrong. I even told him he submarined me. He said he did not and why don't I call him. I was not raised to chase a man down. Men are predators. So, I told him he has a phone too. I know women were throwing themselves at him due to all his success. But that is not my character. I do want to feel desired and wanted. I liked this man and could see us together but chase me because I am a catch too!

I was not raised to chase a man, but my goodness, why would he disappear on me? This happened many times, so I learned not to put any effort into my emotions. I wondered if he had a wife, a secret lover, or many women. I just did not get it. Why would he take me to his home to meet his child? It was not adding up, and I still have not figured it out. I guess he had many options. But what he did not know was so did I—not by choice but by default. I actually liked this man, but I was not in a race to catch him.

I have heard many stories of women getting love bombed. The man acts as if he is all into the woman and has a serious relationship with her. He gets her entangled into his deceptive heart and plays the game like he is going to go all the way then he love bombs her. Some women have even been left at the altar or when they were planning their wedding. It is a ruthless, heartless move but it happening to frequently. It's like guard your heart for real.

Women are almost forced into playing these childish games to protect their heart. So, what many have done is become just as cut throat as the men to keep their sanity. That is just not in my DNA. I need a game less Godly man who is not a narcissist!

Chapter Seven

THE NARCISSIST

I can't write this book and not talk about the narcissist. Webster describes this person as a someone who has an excessive interest in or admiration of themselves. Ladies, I know you have dealt with this type of man before. They can do no wrong. They try to make you think you are at fault and insufficient. The world revolves around them, and sometimes, you can lose yourself in their manipulation. This can be a man or woman. But right now, I am talking about a man. A narcissist can have you questioning who you are. They are cunning and good with convincing people. You can start questioning your value dealing with one as they try to control your moves and even your thoughts.

I was dating a person with these characteristics, and someone told me he was a narcissist. I had no clue of what I was dealing with. I found myself second-guessing myself. I was placating to his every emotion thinking I was doing the right thing. I even took the blame for things I should not have taken the blame for. I was trying to be the better person with humility but had no clue what I was dealing with. More and more of this man's self-centered behavior came out. Everything was to fit his needs. A narcissist does not want to bend. It's their way or the highway. Everyone must cater to them. Ladies, you may find yourselves always giving in because you were tricked out of the apology due to you. Run!

This type of man is controlling, dangerous to your emotions, and loves himself too much. He will destroy you if he can when things don't go his way. He is a master at belittling people. He has the mini-god syndrome. He should date himself. You deserve better. You deserve a man who will not treat you like a child but love you as God's priceless jewel. This type of man can be very short with you, curt, and impatient when you oppose him. I say, run again! He needs a fool not a Proverbs 31 woman. A narcissist cannot appreciate who you are. He spends too much time tearing you down so he can be the center of attraction. It does not matter how beautiful, sweet, and successful you are. A narcissist is a narcissist. Point blank.

Chapter Eight

THE "I CAN'T FUNCTION WITHOUT HIM" SYNDROME

Ladies, don't ever let no man get you to this point. This is when you have a soul tie that needs to be broken! Don't let any relationship steal your joy, goals, finances, business, dignity, or destiny. A man can get you so off track that you find it hard to get focused again. I remember when I was in school trying to be a doctor. I did not want a serious relationship. I knew that if I got too emotionally involved and he cut me off or did something degrading, I would fall apart. I could not jeopardize my schooling over my heart being tied up with someone who could potentially hurt me. So, I became unemotional like a man. Dating with no attachments or heart. This is not natural.

Now that I am as old as I am and in ministry, I really have to be careful. It's a harder fall at this age, and I have much more to lose. I can't sacrifice ministry and all the work God has done with me over the years. He cleaned me up, made me whole, and gave me a purpose. I just can't handle a crucial emotional set back at this point. This is why I need GOD with this. He is the one in the beginning who told Adam to name his wife. He felt Adam needed help, so he put Adam to sleep. Only he can wake him up and give him instructions. So, I need God to intervene and wake up my man.

I have let the wrong Adam try to claim and name me before. It's too costly to make that same mistake again. Many of us have had unnecessary headaches because the wrong Adam named us. The wrong Adam cannot appreciate who you are. He was a counterfeit. So, he names you with the wrong purpose and destiny. Because it was the wrong person, I was trying to fit into his plans that were not God's plan for my life. I was acting if you will because I was not walking in my full potential. I was walking in some other woman's shoes. This man did not know how to value me or recognize all I was carrying. He did not know how to speak life over me or nurture what I had inside of me for my man's vision. My potential was being stifled but I tried to fit in where I did not fit in. Ladies don't do it!

This man could not even cover me because he was not capable. He could not see all that was exposed in my life. He did not have my back or care to have my back. My purpose did not line up with his. I was a stranger he wanted to date for potential marriage. The man is supposed to be your protector, your provider, your friend, your partner and more. Though God is your spiritual covering, this man is supposed to cover you in the natural. I dated men who did not understand my makeup let alone when I was in a battle.

They would try to put me down because I was strong not because I asked for it, I just had to be. It seemed like they wanted to break me or mold me into what they thought I should be. Adam did not change Eve. He named her as God told him to. He did not belittle her. He knew she was pulled from his side, so he instructed her accordingly. He make-up was his makeup. She was part of his bone and flesh. She was his missing piece, for lack of a better word, I thought to myself when I was misappropriated, negro how dare you? I knew I was a great catch and would make some man a great helpmate one day, but he could not see that because he was not the right Adam.

As a minister, when I came up against trials that weighed me down, I settled for a man that did not even know how to pray. I was just tired of being alone. I was trying not to be so demanding and lower my expectations so I could be married. But this made me miserable. I was misunderstood in who I was as God made me to be. My gifts were not appreciated when these were the gifts God gave me to help acquire our destiny together. Ladies don't do this. Down the years, you will be sorry. You find out more about the person you married, and you live a life never fulfilling your dreams. He can't help it; he was not for you. He did not understand how wonderful you are. This caused you to second-guess your own greatness. It's not worth it. Years of my life were lost being tied up with the wrong man. I can't get those years back. But at this older age, I can't afford to make those mistakes again.

Chapter Nine

THE SNAKE, YOU'RE BEING WATCHED

Today, we live in a world where nothing is really a secret. We are tracked, watched, and evaluated from our social media. But the predator is lurking to try to get you in a snare of fake love. Many of them have motives because they see how you move on your social media. I have even had some try to scam me out of money because they thought I was a fool. Men are often looking for a steak momma or come up as well. Many men have asked me to borrow money. They see me on my socials traveling the world and think I am loaded. These men study you so that they know how to approach you.

    Let's think about it. If someone was to watch your Tik Tok, Instagram, or Facebook, it's a matter of time before they know your likes and dislikes. I call these men working for the monitoring spirits. They watch your every move. As sad as it may seem, people can be that cunning. I had a minister calling me who tried to get in my panties and thought he would slither in by meeting my emotional needs. He studied me, so he knew what to say. He knew my hairstyles, my dislikes, etc. to help him go in for the kill. But he was looking for some woman to take care of him. There are so many men like that who want to be kept. I don't mean to be indignant but real. They think their piece is enough. Don't fall for the trap, ladies. You been holding out living a holy life, and the devil sends your type. Once he establishes that sexual soul tie, it's hard to detox him out your system. Trust me, he knows that. But all along, he had an agenda. He knew just what you liked, so he became that to win you over.

This man is dangerous. He will cause you to come out of character because he is foul. You get so wrapped up into him that you become like him to deal with him. He plays the role long enough to win the prize. That's your money, your time, your dignity, your home, your business, your dreams, you name it. Remember he was sent by the devil. The devil is ancient and been here for years, so he knows what you like. He knows how to dress it up so nicely. When you slip or drop your guard because you want to be married or just lonely, that is when he seals the deal. He wants to destroy you and take your self-worth. When you get to that state you become desperate because of the soul tie. No man or person is worth you losing you. That is not the Adam God has for you.

I been tricked by this type of man in one of my low moments. It took a minute to come back around. I thanked God I did not sleep with him because I may have still been trapped now. But this man was so sharp and deceiving that I believed he wanted me for me. NOT! I was his way to success, connections, and elevation. Listen, you women who are successful, if you can get a man who can pour into you, please do so. You all are equal. The Bible calls it equally yoked. That means across the border and not just spiritually. Pray that the Lord sends one that can elevate you and lead you to your destiny.

You are not the head nor are you really supposed to be the provider. You are the helper, that's it. Don't start taking headship over all this man's bills and you not even married yet. God will send you better. It does not take all of that for your Adam. You doing back flips for a man whose plan all along was to ride off of you and your success. This is not a joint venture between the two of you. Both people should bring something together because eventually you are cleaving as one. You should have like minds—and not a mind used to scam the one you *say* you love. Many men do this to women who have it going on. Some of you rich women I hate to say it, Christian or not, may need a prenup.

Watch who approaches you from social media. As stated, they have studied you. It is not a coincident. It was a plot to get to you. I don't care how nice he seems. Don't fall for it! I look at rich actors and singers all the time who fall in love with a man who had his eyes on their estate and in up taking half! I feel for these women. My money right now is nowhere near theirs, but like me, they thought they were in love, too. Many of them worked so hard for their success because they came from very humble beginnings, and they fall in love with someone who had an agenda the whole time. Again, the devil knows what you want and will send it wrapped up in a package that has been studying you.

Chapter Ten

AVOID THESE MEN AT ALL COSTS!

Ladies, ladies, ladies. Now, I am not an expert with men. But I have been through some things. I also talked to my single girlfriends and regardless of the age, it's the same ole problem. I am on an island with only 36 square miles and a young girl named Akeema who told me she was single here because the women here are dealing with the same issues I am. She is 26, and I am old enough to be her mom, but she assured me that it isn't even age-related. Just a hindrance in obtaining positive relationships. Wow. She mentioned to me because the island is so small, it is a greater problem. There are even less men who have an abundance of women to choose from. Ironically like the states, the women are driven by the money. They are losing their standards to have that man.

Who makes up "that man"? Let's examine some of these types.

Let's talk about the man (A) who will go to church to get a church girl. He will pretend to want to know the word until he gets the panties. She thinks she can change him and becomes his Bible study partner. She spends more and more time with him in Bible study and establishes a soul tie even without sex. But what she disregards is he has no plans of getting saved and delivered. This is a dangerous man because he has been sent by the devil with a plot to pull her out of her relationship with God. This is an old trick of the enemy.

Okay, let's go to man (B). He is as charming as he can be. He has no plans of ever settling down. He will have children, date you, and treat you like a queen. But he has many queens and children with them. He has a rotation system, and he treats them all as if one day he will settle down, and they are his main chick. But the reality is if you let him run that game, he will. Just because he gives you money and comes by on the child's birthday does not mean he will settle down. These women waste countless years wondering when will they ever get married. They know there has to be someone else, but they don't care. They want to win the prize and be the one he chooses. But is it really winning a prize? This man will break your heart. He has learned how to spread his emotions thin. Yes, the baby gets new shoes and the latest outfits, but you never get this man's heart. He gives you just enough to hope and stay in the picture.

Exhibit (C) man—The polished man who has the money for real fits in this category. He normally wants the perfect woman but will fondle your heart. He knows his money is his attraction. He does not have to be fine because he is loaded. He expects you to lower your standards because he knows multiple women would do anything to be with him. He does not value you but definitely has a bed agenda. Now when he does slow down, he usually gets a bombshell who is younger than him and who runs a game on him. He does not care because she looks good on his arm. But the woman with the mental stamina of him who has her own program together is too much for him. She does not need him, but she wants him. That type of women who is self-sufficient is too exhausting for him. She usually is not going to take his mess but for so long, so it does not work. This man ultimately wants a hospice nurse wife who will take care of him when his money can't. But little does he know that she will have a man on the side spending up his money until he dies and leaves it all to her.

The men of the cloth are something else. Bishops, apostles, pastors, prophets, and ministers, sometimes, are as bad as the ones in the street. They are exhibit (D). They use the church as a front. They pretend to be holy but have slept with half of the young women in the church. Their wife is aware, but she prefers to close her eyes, turn her cheeks, and stay the first lady. After all, it's the prestige of the title. As a minister of the gospel, unfortunately, I have come in contact with the sex in the pulpit mentality. I have had instances when I was new to the ministry that almost made me run away from ministry.

Case in point, I remember I was working on a play in Alabama, and I met a pastor who had scoped me out when I was interviewing on the radio to promote the play. One of the announcers said this man wanted to meet me. Now, I was new to ministry and thought ok no problem. I thought he needed info on the play. Well, that was not the case. Since I did not have a rental car, the radio personality said the pastor would drop me off at my hotel.

I thought, *Ok, he can't be that crazy because the radio station knew he offered.* But this man drove me all around Birmingham and took me to his church saying I was the missing piece. Now, I thought he was crazy. I just wanted to go to my hotel. Eventually, he took me, and I thought I was done with him.

However, The next day, an early Sunday morning, he came in my room. He paid the maid to let him in. Unbelievable. Now I said Sunday morning, y'all. I was in my slinky pajamas in my room when he walked in. He was suited down on his way to his early-morning service. I by all means threatened him with calling authorities if he did not get out. So, he left, but for the rest of my stay, I had security. Now that was a man in clergy.

Let me give you another encounter. I was in Cleveland promoting another play and met many pastors. They all had my number to give them promo tickets. Well, a very prominent pastor called me at 3 a.m. saying to touch my chest because he wanted to pray with me. He proceeded to start praying and breathing rapidly. I thought, *Lord, what have I gotten myself into?* I hung up on him and told him he was crazy. I was to drop off his tickets that Sunday and speak to his church about the play. Thank God, I did not go alone because I was escorted back into his office by his assistant. I could see pictures of his family on the shelf behind him. But he proceeded to say in front of his armourbearer and my friend that he wanted to connect with me later that day after church. He had his armourbearer close the door with us in the office. His assistant did not seem alarmed, so I was sure this had happened with some other ladies who would go for it. I told him he might not want to mess with me because I would go out in the pulpit and tell the people what type of pastor they served. I would have turned that church upside down and exposed him if I got on that pulpit. By all means, I was not the one. He eventually left me alone, and I left him his tickets.

The counterfeit man (exhibit E) is busy, y'all. He is the man looking for a jig aloo experience. He pretends to have what he does not have. He is clean now with his nice watch, clean shoes, and latest outfit. But he is broke! His time is spent trying to present his suave looks and style to women with money. His whole check goes to his outfit. He often approaches older women who have been single for a while. He thinks they are desperate. This happens in the church, too. I have had my fair share ask me for money because they thought I was banking. They did not want to spend theirs but wanted to spend mines.

But many of these men go after the well-off business woman or the retired women with a pension or two. HE IS AN OPPORTUNIST AND WANTS YOUR CONNECTIONS TO COME UP! His smooth-talking, wining, and dining disposition last only until he seals the deal; it's how he flows. Sometimes, he will even expect the woman to pay the bills once he has moved in. She loves him, so she does not mind, and little does she know he loves her money. He will play the game, establish himself off her riches, and milk her for all she has. He will even marry her because he is looking for security in its longevity capacity. He slides right on in until he is a part of everything. At that point, he uses her and does what he wants because he is in there, claiming her respect and climbing the ladder that *she* built. Now, he is part of her socialite company. Guess what? It's cheaper to keep him because he will take half. He is trifling and would sue.

This is not a real man. I have seen this so many times with actors. He is a master con artist!

This next—man, oh my. His mom can be your nightmare. Let's talk about man (F), the momma's boy. He might as well marry his mother. She does not want to let him go, and no woman is good enough for him in her eyes. Some of these mothers did not have a man in the home, and so, keep the son on close watch. It's been him as the father of the household. In other cases, the son was just spoiled rotten. He could do no wrong. The mother babied him to the point where she even washed his clothes as an adult. She hindered him. She did what it took to keep him around except intimate gestures. She made it miserable for the girlfriend, fiancé or even the wife.

This man would call his momma with every little problem in his relationship. Sometimes when mad at his wife, he would spend the night at momma's house thus making the wife look bad. Well into his late thirties, momma was still babying him. Momma's stop! You raised men who are inadequate and who are not really self-sufficient. So, these men never wake up into true manhood and appreciate their wives the way they should appreciate them. The wife becomes the second woman of the house. Don't let mom move in; it's over then. The wife is hindered in her wifely helper duties because momma feels she can always do it better. Clean better, cook better and just take care of her son better.

Men, stop being big babies and be the man God called you to be as the head of the household. Lovingly, direct your mom to her place so your marriage is not ruined. Remember the Bible says for a man to leave his parents and cleave to his wife. Genesis 2:24 states this and is repeated in the New Testament in Matthew 19:5 and Ephesians 5:31. Check it out for comparison.

Genesis 2:24: "Therefore a man shall leave his father and his mother and hold fast to his wife, and they shall become one flesh."

Matthew 19:5: Jesus quotes Genesis, stating, "For this cause a man shall leave his father and mother and shall cleave to his wife, and the two shall become one flesh."

Ephesians 5:31: "For this reason a man will leave his father and mother and be united to his wife, and the two will become one flesh."

This concept of "leaving and cleaving" means a husband establishes a new, primary family unit with his wife, prioritizing their marital relationship, and forming a deep, lifelong bond, rather than a complete abandonment of his parents according to many Bible study guides.

There are so many different aspects of today's man. I am going to just talk about these I have mentioned and exhibit (G). Ooh this man scares me. He is prettier than you and his nails are cleaner than yours. He is fine, built and he knows it. Whether he has money or not, he plays with your life. Why because he knows he is respectable with a great career but on the down low. This man will marry you, go to church or not go to church but have a man on the side. He meets him at the gym. That is his bestie. But this man can act as if he hates the lifestyle and people in it. Well, that is just a decoy.

He will raise children, come home, provide but have another life. Women go for years and years until one day the sin catches up with him. Neighbors, friends, and family question his masculinity but many times the wife is blind.

Or just maybe she does not want to break up the family. It's sad, but I see a lot of this in the church as well as among very successful business men. Many ladies just ride it out knowing their husband really wants what they want. Lord, we must pray for sure because women have died staying in situations like this. That spirit of deception can cause an unexpected end. Ladies, get out! Most likely, he has made up his decision and is not changing. Get Your Dignity Back!

Chapter Eleven

WHY DOES HE STILL CALL YOU?

Women, you may ask why does he still call you when you both know he runs from commitment. Well, let me help you out. He calls you because you have something special that others may lack. He knows that you are a great woman that God pieced together, so he does not want to let you go. He may not tell you that he is keeping you in close proximity because he is trying to figure things out. Your very existence and persona illuminates the spirit of a good woman, and he knows that. He does not want to lose you, so he keeps you at arm's length. I know it is unfair because he may not be quite honest about his intentions.

But who wants to be available at his disposal while he is rotating women? He is trying to see who he will really want to commit to. No one has time to be an option. Unless you have no desire to be in a serious relationship yourself, this type of vibe can pull at your emotions. He is all in one week, and the next week, you can't figure it out. I know when this kept happening to me, many of my friends said just date, too, with your own rotation. I thought no I can't do that. I am a pastor, but they said this way my feelings would not get tied up in what I thought could have been a serious courtship leading to marriage. Eventually, I had to learn to hold myself back and not allow myself to get too caught up when men were trying to court me.

Many times, I told God this is unnatural because I feel like I am putting up a front and not being my loving self to protect my emotions. Personally, I don't like this type of dating because I am waiting for God to really bless me with whom he designed for me. This type of dating keeps you from being authentic because you are often withholding how you really feel, which is sad. It's a dating cycle where you have to pretend to not be that into the man. This is so you don't get burnt emotionally. Instead of him saying I am dating others or weighing out my options, he gives you false hope. He calls you just enough to keep you in the loop. It's almost like he has a timer and knows when you are about to bounce, so he calls.

Well, I know I have bounced totally in the past if he could not figure it out. I did not stay to have myself on the chopping board where it would take months or years to get my emotions back intact. No, I am too old for these games. Been there, done that. The man God has for me needs to know that I am his rib, his helper, and he can't do without me. Why, because I am part of his purpose and his destiny. Ladies, we have to know our value, too, and what we bring to the table. Being in rotation can make you second-guess you.

This is all too crazy to me, but this is how it is. Men have so many options, and they make each option feel like they are potentially the one why they figure it out.

Men, go before the Lord! He will give you the answer. Don't tie up a woman who deserves to be properly cherished and loved.

Women, we are typically more emotional beings, so if he does a few things right, we ready to jump in. But little do we know that oftentimes, he is doing that with his rotational schedule of women. You are all of that and a bag of chips, and he still has you in rotation. He knows you are a good thing and have it going on, so to keep you, he plays mind games, giving you just enough. Don't allow his indecisiveness make you question your value. You know you are the apple of God's eyes and a queen, so don't minimize who you are with his ambivalence.

Ladies, this type of man is not candid with where he is. He will drag you along as your emotions become more involved and then pick someone else in the lineup. I personally got to a point where I said if you are not courting and seeking God for a potential mate, then I am not the one. I'd rather spare me than be a part of a dating pool for any man. Maybe that is why I am single now and still waiting. I am just too old to be in rotation. I need a secure man who knows what he wants and, without hesitation, goes after it. As a godly woman, I need a man who can lead me as the head as God directs him.

A man that is indecisive and unstable can also be a very insecure man. Sometimes, you are so dynamic that they cannot handle who you are though they want you. So why they are trying to figure it out, they can make you seem insecure, questioning who you really are. It's a game, ladies. Never doubt or minimize who God made you to be.

The Bible says in Psalms 139:13-16 KJV:

> For thou hast possessed my reins: Thou hast covered me in my mother's womb. I will praise thee; for I am fearfully and wonderfully made: Marvellous are thy works; And that my soul knoweth right well. My substance was not hid from thee, When I was made in secret, and curiously wrought in the lowest parts of the earth.

So never forget how fabulous you are as God's art piece.

God uniquely designed you for some man that will appreciate all your gifts and talents without him being intimidated. Remember that man who has you in rotation can't even deny to himself how wonderful you are, which is why he keeps you close. His own boys can see that you are a good woman. Many ask, "Man, when you gonna lock that down?" Sometimes, the man's fear or the spirit of intimidation causes him to lose a great woman. Let that man know who you are as a daughter of the almighty king and you are indeed waiting on the king who is your earthly king. You are waiting on a man who knows who he is and what he wants based on what God has told him. He is not afraid to take that leap with you and respect and adorn who you are because he can see you are an asset and not a liability. You are his missing piece.

Therefore, you are too much of a jewel to be a part of any rotational system. Let him figure it out, but you keep soaring and being the great woman God intended for you to be. The right man who values you will find you.

Chapter Twelve

WOMEN, WHAT HAPPENS WHEN THE RIGHT MAN SHOWS UP?

Listen, ladies, you have been praying and waiting for that man. Don't let your encounter when you meet him be your last. I am not saying walk on egg shells, but you have been preparing for this. So, check your attitude, your baggage of all past hurt, and those soul ties. Make sure you do not bring the ex-drama into your new relationship. Even if you see something that may resemble your ex, pray and make sure God said this is your man. Pray for this man, too. No relationship is perfect, so it can have some unexpected challenges. Cover your future husband in prayer. If God says tell no one, then tell no one. The enemy would want nothing more than to break the covenant before it starts.

Another piece of advice is to not let your girlfriends know how good or bad it is going. You do not need anyone else's bad baggage in your new relationship because they are unhappy. Be careful who you take advice from. Everybody's relationships is different. Some are even jealous because you finally found your great Adam. Don't let your girlfriend talk you out of your blessing when God finally woke your Adam up! Women can spill their hurt into your situation. You can self-sabotage your destiny, too, by listening and reacting to the wrong voice of advice. Don't do it. Be that Proverbs 31 woman God speaks of so that when your man sees you, he knows he won the prize. Maintain a sweet aroma to God's nostrils. Your Adam will sniff you to see if you have his smell. Remember he has been sleeping while God was perfecting you. You should not smell like any other man, but your man God decided for you. After all, you came from his side as his missing rib!

Don't wait until he wakes up to try to get it together. You have had years of waiting. Many times, you thought of going back to your ex just to be with a man. So have that hair tight, body right, makeup laid, credit intact, business on point, and attitude godly. Prepare to be his wife. By all means, please don't be a nagger or a very argumentative woman. In Proverbs 21:9 (KJV), it states, "It is better to dwell in a corner of the housetop [i.e., an attic] than with a brawling woman in a wide house."

Ladies, don't bring this into your relationship. A man likes a gentle, humble, sweet woman who understands he is dealing with a lot, too. After all, he has been sleeping for a long time. So, when he wakes up and is ready to speak life over you with naming you, he does not want all the bickering and nagging. Be loving and let him know what he was missing by dreaming so long.

Chapter Thirteen

ARE YOU AUTHENTICALLY YOU?

Ladies, your man finally woke up, and he is looking for you. Are you the DNA representative of who God created you to be? Or are you a bitter woman who picked up toxicity in your attitude? Maybe because you thought it would never happen. Somebody got in your head and discouraged you. Or just maybe you thought you were too old now. You are right at the brink of meeting your dream man but decided, "You know what? I don't need a man" because you were tired of waiting. I have seen this happen to so many women because they gave up waiting for that man God had for them. They were tired of the counterfeits and decided maybe they were just going to do them and have fun. So, they develop a cold, emotionless disposition to just date frivolously.

Women who have had bad relationships and been taken advantage of in their past often say they are just going to date like men. They convince themselves they don't need a man anymore, or they will have many. They have embraced singleness when God was about to bless them in that next hour. Their attitude got so jaded due to past hurt that they walk in a person their friends told them to be to protect their heart. Ladies, regardless of past hurt, at some point, you have to open up to receive that man God has for you. You have to be willing to put your heart out there again and trust that with prayer, this man came from the Lord.

Many women get so used to being alone that often times they convince themselves that they will never have no one, so they might as well date like men do. They leave the emotions out of the picture. Once an open, soft, and loving woman becomes callous, closed, and passive about a man that could be a good man. At this point of bitterness, all men are the same. This woman has lost her true identity and is now in protective mode. So, when the right one shows up, she does not know how to embrace whom God has sent her. She messes up or almost sabotages what could be her beautiful future. Been there, done that. I had not given the relationship a chance because I had already thought it would fail due to past relationships. My attitude was nonchalant, which is not who God made me to be.

But on another note, the man shows up and the woman did not present who she really is. He is looking for whom God showed him or who he sees as his soul mate. If you play games with him when he is ready, you can run the chance of losing him. He is looking for your authentic self. The kind, beautiful woman who watched from a far. He no longer wants to play games because he is looking for his wife. He is looking for his favor as the Bible says in Proverbs 18:22 NIV: "He who finds a wife finds what is good and receives favor from the LORD." But, ladies, if we camouflage who we are because we are scared to get hurt, we can miss whom God has for us. I am not saying don't be cautious and put your heart out there to be cut up. But do open up and be yourself. Drop the facade so your future mate can see who he thought you were. Pray and ask God if he is the one. Then once you get the green light to move forward, be who you really are and not who you think he wants you to be or who your friends told you to be. He already has an idea of his future wife's persona. Don't miss it by being tired, scared, or pretending to be who the world told you to be. Be that kind, gentle woman you are. If he is really from God, he will not mishandle you.

A godly man knows what he needs and wants. After all, he has been asleep as God dropped nuggets in his spirit to prepare him to meet you when he wakes up. He needs to wake up with a plan and find the woman who is his rib. If you pretend to be who you are not or another rib, then Mr. Right may think you don't fit the vision. Be who God authentically made you to be and don't be afraid to let him in.

Chapter Fourteen

WHEN A MAN LOVES YOU AND TREATS YOU RIGHT

To all who are reading this, please note when a man cherishes a woman and treats her right, there is nothing she will not do for her man. The right man sent by God will speak life over her, protect, love, provide, pray with her, encourage her, and by all means not break her spirit. She is the apple of his eye. He has her on the brain and yearns to see and speak to her daily. He wants more than just a texting relationship. The sound of her voice excites his soul. He will nurture her and forgive her when she is wrong. This man will let her know what he loves about her and adores her attributes. A true godly man is not afraid to tell a woman how dynamic she really is. He feels blessed he got the prize. He would never belittle his woman or expose her shortcomings. This is a real man. Where the woman is weak, he will pick up the pieces and help build her up. A godly secure man knows his soon-to-be wife is his missing link, and he is happy he found her. Wow. His emotions are not hidden, but he speaks of his love in the timing of God. He does not want to lead the woman on or move out of order. He is careful to not hurt his woman's feelings and is sensitive to her needs. What a man, what a man.

The right man wants to see you excel. He is not trying to change all the wonderful attributes about you but cherish them. He knows God gave you all of those gifts to help with his vision. You are supposed to be his helper, so he welcomes all you bring to the table. An insecure man will try to beat you down and make you second-guess yourself. But the man God has for you will love you into your greatness. He is your biggest fan and will push you to succeed. After all, you two are working together as one for a purpose and goal.

Now, ladies, we know if you are loved right, you will go to bat for your man. If you wait for God to bring you your once sleeping Adam with all these attributes, you know you would melt like butter. The counterfeit man did not know how to appreciate how fabulous you really are. He wanted to mold you into someone else when you are the missing rib from the right rib cage. The man with the right rib cage is not going to harm himself. You as a future wife is bone of his bone and flesh of his flesh. He is secure as a real man. He knows if he loves you right and you do not become a scorned woman; there is nothing you two can't conquer together. So, wait on God to wake up that Adam.

And men, don't try to tear down what God has given you when you find her.

Chapter Fifteen

IT IS NOT A COMPETITION BETWEEN YOU AND YOUR ADAM

This topic here I know too well. Men have approached me because they said I had it going on. I think I am ok in the looks, but I really try to take care of myself. I eat right and think of positive things. I pray and fast as much as I can, and I am responsible. I have compassion for people, and I am a natural born helper. But men who are not the real Adam approach me because they like the fact that I am intelligent and seem to have a great career. But when they find out I have a brain for real and God is elevating me, they begin to hate me for what attracted them to me.

Case in point. I am a woman in ministry. I did not ask for it, it just happened because God called me. I have been blessed to be made an Apostle. Now, I am not caught up in all of that and barely wear my robes. But men who want to be my Adam are. Many men in ministry have tried to knock me down as if we are in a competition. They were drawn to my accomplishments but wanted to rename me to be docile and act as if God had not done all he did for me. One pastor told me if we get together what would they call me when married. He said that because I am an apostle. Well, ladies in ministry, don't get it twisted. Your godly true Adam is the head of your home. You don't bring all that positioning into the marriage. This goes for boss ladies, too, who may have many employees to oversee, but your Adam is not one of them. Adam sent by God will value and appreciate who you are. All that you accomplished is to help with the vision for the two of you. By no means are you all in competition with each other. You are a team. Let him know that.

However, sometimes the Adams are intimidated by your strength and accomplishments, especially if it seems that you are more accomplished than he may be. If that is your man from God, you have to assure him that you are not on a game show and in competition. Let him know that due to his insecurities, he found you so that you can be his helper not on the opposing team. Pray and ask God how to help him put things in perspective so you two do not lose out on a great situation. Many men have made me feel so insecure because they were not the right Adam. They thought my accomplishments were something they could handle. But, ladies, the right Adam will know just what to do with you and how to multiply off of all you have done for you all's joint purpose.

Chapter Sixteen

A Momma's Boy Versus a Mother's Love

Ladies, ladies, ladies, the momma's boy, a man who is still stuck to his mother's bosom, hard to break, date, and marry. Many times, wives and girlfriends are second to Momma. Now, I am not saying that a man should not love his mother, respect her, or put his girlfriend before his mom. But I am saying she does not come before his wife. The Bible says to leave and cleave in Genesis 2:24 KJV: "Therefore shall a man leave his father and his mother, and shall cleave unto his wife: and they shall be one flesh." So, this means this man is now united with his wife as his own body. So, he is no longer one with his mother as he once was when she carried him. Just because a godly whole man recognizes his wife as now his own flesh does not mean he does not love his mother. However, a man who has it twisted or has been manipulated by his mother is not an Adam that is ready to become one with his future wife.

This man does not know his true identity because he is looking for his woman to be his mother. These men are tough to break from that cycle. Ladies, you are not called to be your Adam's momma. Some men can't find their wives because they are looking for their mother in their soon-to-be wives. They are often drawn to their mother's characteristics when pursuing a mate, but what if God chiseled out a totally different make up for his wife? If he is not awakened, he will miss her because he is trying to mold a woman who has already been molded by God to help him.

This type of men is blinded to comparing every woman to their mother. They are sleeping for sure because they have not allowed God to define who they are, and thus, they function like little boys when they are supposed to be the man the woman relies on.

God defined Adam. He gave him instructions for Eve and said he would make him a helpmate. Adam was the man. He had already worked and named every living creature on earth before Eve came to be. Then Adam named Eve. Genesis 2:20 states,

> *So the man gave names to all the livestock, the birds in the sky and all the wild animals. But for Adam no suitable helper was found. 21 So the Lord God caused the man to fall into a deep sleep; and while he was sleeping, he took one of the man's ribs and then closed up the place with flesh. 22 Then the Lord God made a woman from the rib[h] he had taken out of the man, and he brought her to the man". 23 The man said, "This is now bone of my bones and flesh of my flesh; she shall be called 'woman,' for she was taken out of man.*

God did not tell him when he woke up his helper was his mother made from his rib. She is the rib from his father. This type of man needs to stay asleep until he can recognize his wife for who she is so that he does not force her to step out of her role as his helper.

These men run to Momma every time there is an argument with the spouse or soon-to-be helpmate. His mother sometimes thinks there is no woman good enough for her forty-year-old baby boy, so this man is mesmerized by his mother's ideology and will come to believe that no woman can to meet his standards. Wake up, sir! Your momma does not want you to leave her, especially when the father of the house is deceased, imprisoned, or has ghosted the mother. She really relies on her son to take the positioning of the father. This is dangerous. The son now placates to his mom's every cry whether it's genuine or manipulative. Mothers, if you are doing this, stop so your son can find a healthy relationship at some point with the woman God created for him.

So, what happens to the woman waiting on her Adam when she runs into the momma's boy? Well, if not careful, she begins to second-guess herself because she can never seem to please this man. She takes on the role of his mother and not a potential helpmate. She has stepped out of character and often babies him similar to a mother's love with her child. These men are so used to their mom picking up the pieces that they never mature into the man God called them to be. As long as the woman continues to act as if she is his mother and not his helper, she perpetuates the problem. A real godly man wants his helpmate. Afterall, God woke up the man and told him to name his wife. How can this man do so when he has already named her his new mother?

Women beware of the momma's boy, and make sure you keep your senses, heart, and God's word open to see the man who is *truly* your Adam.

Chapter Seventeen

TAKE OFF THAT OTHER LADY'S CLOTHES

Ladies, whose clothes are you wearing? In other words, what woman of your Adam's past is taunting your future? Has the counterfeit Adam made you so insecure that you put on the cloak of a woman he once loved? A man who constantly brings up his past relationship or often rekindles his contact with his ex is not your Adam. Your Adam has been delivered and is free to now find his true love. A godly man has been purged of all soul ties and is liberated to name and claim his wife. He does not constantly bring up his past into his new relationship. Obviously, it did not work because you are now in the picture.

But now, instead of realizing your worth, you strip away your authenticity and dress in her ways just to appease him. Don't do it! Be whom God made you to be, and if he can't see that, he may not be for you. I see so many beautiful, talented women degraded by a man's comparison to his ex. These women are progressive and great catches, but this type of man can't see it. He is stuck in his past though he wants a new future. He cannot appreciate whom God brought into his life, so he mishandles an awesome woman of God.

Ladies, I know you have been there. So do not dumb down or even deviate from the awesomeness God created you with. Once God gives you that spiritual and natural DNA, that's it. There is some man who recognizes you as his rib, and he has been missing you. When men constantly compare you to their past, it can create insecurities. Soon after, you may begin to dress in the cloak of someone else. If he likes a certain type of perfume his ex used to wear, then you might buy that same perfume to please him. If he liked her hairdo, then you might switch up your hair, hoping he notices. If she was skinnier, oh my, then you will try to lose weight. Sometimes, a man will try to conform you into what he used to like. But if it is your Adam, he will cherish all your beauty and nurture you as you are. Right now.

He will speak life over you and all your gifts. He knows God anointed you with special talents to help him fulfill his vision. He does not try to reinvent you to be someone else. Don't change who you are to coerce him into adoring you. The right man for you will appreciate your goodness and beauty. God crafted you to be how you are for his kingdom purposes. If you try to walk in someone else's shoes, you just may attract and get the Adam that is not for you. Don't even covet anyone else's swag. God has a swag for you that makes you unique. Too many times, women think less of themselves because they may not be a twin to his past girlfriend. Or just maybe one of his friends told you that you are not his typical type, so you start doubting.

Please women of God, don't belittle your purpose for the Adam you are not purposed for. Bite the bullet and move on because obviously this one is still sleeping and wants to make you into his fairytale princess.

You are royalty in a linen outfit according to God. Every last one of your hairs are numbered. God designed you to his perfection. He did not design you to look and act exactly like someone else. If he wants a woman who is five-foot-nine and looks like a runway model, but you are five-two, he may not ever be totally satisfied. Now, if he is mature enough in the Lord, and the Lord says you are the one, he will not find the same level of true happiness if he disobeys. So, by all means, you are a masterpiece of God, and you need to remember that while you are waiting on your Adam. You are in God's museum, and it is a privilege for him to have you. You are a priceless masterpiece that cannot be brought but gifted by God to the Adam deserving of you.

Chapter Eighteen

GOD, MY BODY IS CHANGING, PLEASE SEND MY ADAM!

I can remember when I was in my twenties and thirties; I could eat anything and still have a dope body. Sometimes, I did not worry about the future state of my body. I would freeze the house out with my air condition, not thinking of my bones in the future. Though a health freak, I would occasionally spaz out on eating a bunch of junk when a life crisis hit me. I partied all night, not worrying about my looks of bags in the future. People kept telling me once I approached thirty-five my metabolism would change. I now know what they were talking about. I have always been an athlete, but in between bad relationships, I often lost myself. Eating some chips or chocolate ice-cream when depressed was a no-brainer to me.

But I was youthful, so I could jump right back. I thought why on earth did I let some man drive me to eat like I could care less. Well, it was a depressed glutton spirit that came upon me. Trust me, gluttony is in the Bible, too. See Philippians 3:18-19:

> *For many walk, of whom I have told you often, and now tell you even weeping, that they are the enemies of the cross of Christ: whose end is destruction, whose god is their belly, and whose glory is their shame-who set their mind on earthly things.*

Overeating, as I would do eventually, could cause shame and disappointment in oneself. When I picked up weight, affecting my body, I brought the shame on myself. Don't go there, ladies! Call a friend you can trust to pray you through it. Here is another one of my favorites scriptures from Proverbs 23:2 KJV: *And put a knife to thy throat, if thou be a man given to appetite.* Whoowee, this one stopped me from over-indulging and disfiguring me in my bad relationships or just in life. I figured out at some point that my body is a temple from God, and I was mishandling it, which would cause aches and pains in the future.

But anyway, I just stopped caring about me when rejected, neglected, or mishandled with the wrong Adam I liked. As fine as people said I was, I did not think so. So now I had pain, shame, depression, low self-worth, and a body changing all at the same time. Can you identify? Many of my low moments were accompanied with not working out, which compounded the situation. I thought why even do all of this? I was still single, and the men I was dating were still tripping. I began to have to speak life over me and let no human being dictate my health, stamina, or who I am. But athlete or not, over the years, "Life be Lifeng!"

So, you notice yourself creeping past forty and single, creeping past fifty and single, and sometimes sixty. There are many women who were once married to the wrong man, hello, and now find themselves single yet again. They desire to get it right this time with God's guidance, so they wait on God. But due to all the wear and tear on their bodies, they also find themselves fighting just to stay healthy. These women have finally figured out their value and who they really are, but the body has started declining. Hair begins to grey, stiffness often sets in, menopause happens, wrinkles appear, and their youth has now passed them. They overcame sicknesses over the years from the stress of being a mom at some point or from the stress of life. But these ladies, otherwise, are solid. They know how to be with a husband, they have wisdom, they have matured into God's Proverbs 31 woman, but their best healthy years seem to be behind them. Actually, some of these women wasted many years in being connected to the wrong Adam who drained the life out of them. They had to regroup and pick themselves back up to become restored and function.

So, now they may be in their fifties, but their Adam is stuck on the hospice wife mentality I mentioned earlier. In other words, these men may not want a mature woman. So, what does this woman who still has love in her and desires to be with her Adam do? Well one thing is to never think someone will not value you as their queen. When God sends the right one, he will speak life over you.

Secondly, keep your body, mind, and health in the best possible shape you can. You are still alive. There are some women in their sixties who look forty because they have figured it out. They did not give up on God. They did not doubt what God could do. They are holding on to the hope, knowing that God recognizes their body has changed. Don't be like Sarah. She laughed at God when he said he wanted to bless her with a baby in her very old age.

> *12 Therefore Sarah laughed within herself, saying, After I am waxed old shall I have pleasure, my lord being old also? 13 And the Lord said unto Abraham, Wherefore, did Sarah laugh, saying, Shall I of a surety bear a child, which am old? 14 Is anything too hard for the Lord? At the time appointed I will return unto thee, according to the time of life, and Sarah shall have a son* (Genesis 18:12-15 KJV).

I am sure you questioned God, too, like me as your body was changing. But like the good book says, there is NOTHING too hard for God!

Now I am not saying you want a baby, but what I am saying is God can regenerate your tired bones. He can replenish your feminine organs and make you pleasurable to your Adam when he comes. God is a miracle worker. We even see older ladies having babies these days. So, who knows what God can do. Ladies, don't give up on you because the clock is ticking, and your body hurts. God will renew your strength. You must renew your mind to believe that your later years shall be your greater!

Unfortunately, many women as they wait for their Adam are made aware of their age by the world around them. Nothing is geared toward the older woman. She is valued by her youth in and out the church. God can restore back to you as it says in Joel 2 KJV:

> *And I will restore to you the years that the locust hath eaten, the cankerworm, and the caterpillar, and the palmerworm, my great army which I sent among you. 26 And ye shall eat in plenty, and be satisfied, and praise the name of the Lord your God, that hath dealt wondrously with you: and my people shall never be ashamed. 27 And ye shall know that I am in the midst of*

Israel, and that I am the Lord your God, and none else: and my people shall never be ashamed.

Everything that was snatched from you regarding your life and health can be restored. If you have diabetes, change your eating habits. If you have high blood pressure, lose weight and stop all the salt and junk. If you have cancer or had it, God is still a healer. By all means, you are connected to a kingdom clock not a clock of this world. Never let anyone intimidate you out of your promise because of your age. Your bones may ache and crack because you are older, but God can massage those bones and tell you what to do to get back in optimum health. If you don't believe me, check out Ezekiel who spoke to the dry bones in the Bible. Ezekiel 37 KJV reads,

> *37 "The hand of the Lord was upon me, and carried me out in the spirit of the Lord, and set me down in the midst of the valley which was full of bones, 2 And caused me to pass by them round about: and, behold, there were very many in the open valley; and, lo, they were very dry. 3 And he said unto me, Son of man, can these bones live? And I answered, O Lord God, thou knowest. 4 Again he said unto me, Prophesy upon these bones, and say unto them, O ye dry bones, hear the word of the Lord. 5 Thus saith the Lord God unto these bones; Behold, I will cause breath to enter into you, and ye shall live: 6 And I will lay sinews upon you, and will bring up flesh upon you, and cover you with skin, and put breath in you, and ye shall live; and ye shall know that I am the Lord. 7 So I prophesied as I was commanded: and as I prophesied, there was a noise, and behold a shaking, and the bones came together, bone to his bone. 8 And when I beheld, lo, the sinews and the flesh came up upon them, and the skin covered them above: but there was no breath in them. 9 Then said he unto me, Prophesy unto the wind, prophesy, son of man, and say to the wind, Thus, saith the Lord*

God; Come from the four winds, O breath, and breathe upon these slain, that they may live. 10 So I prophesied as he commanded me, and the breath came into them, and they lived, and stood up upon their feet, an exceeding great army.

Speak to your dry bones and command them to wake up in Jesus Christ the Yeshua's name! God did it for these dry bones that were slayed by life, so he can do it for yours. I know because I been there. I have to make myself work out and eat right even if my knees are bothering me. I ask God every day, keep my youthful flow because when my Adam claims me, I want to be in the best possible shape I can be in. Afterall, I did not practice celibacy and holiness all these years to not please my man or be pleasured by him.

So, ladies, take care of you! I know we have all made some bad decisions in the past that have had repercussions on our health. Being depressed can cause all types of issues. But you have a chance to get it together now! Your Adam wants you in great health as you want him to be. You want to enjoy this man you have been waiting for so long. God hears your cry, so trust God's process. Don't sit around and lose the youthfulness you still have left though you are in your fifties. Hit that gym, eat right, and curve that body up with sex appeal. You may be saved, but you're still a woman. God created your body, so he knows all the stages of maturing. He also knows how to redeem the time on your life and give you back that youthful glow you once had. Do your part and don't give up on you because the world said it's too late. Don't let your age and your health permeate into your dress either. In other words, don't be defeated and start looking like some old hopeless woman even in your attire. Rise up and find your youthful you across the border!

I started graying at the age of twelve, and I am still gray. But there was a time where I was so quick to run to the dye bottle until God said stop! The world made me feel old. I almost got sucked up into the lie and gave up on me as my age and hair kept changing. Now single, well over fifty, with white hair but finally confident, I'm told that my white hair is a trademark, my signature, and it's distinguish looking. Young people call me Storm, and the world has caught up with the white hair trend. When I finally accepted the changes that was happening with me and still loved me, then I could do what I needed to do for my body. You cannot let the aches, pains, world mentality, or even your mindset keep you from building up you. Regardless of being single and mature, continue to work on you so your Adam knows you are a preserved fine wine. God kept you, and you don't look or move as an old unhealthy person. God can rebrand your stamina. Your Adam will know it was God that rejuvenated you and kept you just for him! It's never too late, ladies, to be in the best health you can be at an older age. Nor is it too late to get your groove back for your Adam.

Chapter Nineteen

ARE YOU PREPARED FOR YOUR ADAM LIKE ESTHER?

When it was time for Esther to meet her king, she had put everything on the line for her kingdom assignment, and now, it was time to be presented. This is why though it hurts sometimes, the Bible tells us to maximize our singleness as believers. See 1st Corinthians 7:32-34:

> *32 But I would have you without carefulness. He that is unmarried careth for the things that belong to the Lord, how he may please the Lord: 33 But he that is married careth for the things that are of the world, how he may please his wife. 34 There is difference also between a wife and a virgin. The unmarried woman careth for the things of the Lord, that she may be holy both in body and in spirit: but she that is married careth for the things of the world, how she may please her husband.*

Ladies, trust me, I have maximized mine and accepted that when my Adam comes, things will change. I must then concentrate on the things of a married woman. So, I have already prepared my mind to receive my visionary for the house. The right Adam, your king, won't steer you wrong.

Anyway, Esther, like the other women, had to be purified to be presented before the king. Read the story in Esther 2 of the Bible. Here is a peek starting at verse 15:

Now when the turn of Esther, the daughter of Abihail the uncle of Mordecai, who had taken her for his daughter, was come to go in unto the king, she required nothing but what Hegai the king's chamberlain, the keeper of the women, appointed. And Esther obtained favor in the sight of all them that looked upon her. 16 So Esther was taken unto king Ahasuerus into his house royal in the tenth month, which is the month Tebeth, in the seventh year of his reign. 17 And the king loved Esther above all the women, and she obtained grace and favor in his sight more than all the virgins; so that he set the royal crown upon her head, and made her queen instead of Vashti.

But my question is, have you been cleansed and purified so when your Adam finally wakes up, you can receive favor from him, too? There was not a request that Esther made to her king that he did not grant. However, Esther did not require as much fragrances as the other ladies because she had been kept to meet her Adam. She did not dibble and dabble with the wrong Adam, creating a lot of soul ties. She was a virgin in her mind and body. But let's be real, some of us are no virgins…but are reclaimed virgins by God. We had to ask God to strip us of all the negativity that was deposited in us so we could be found. That was part of our purification process.

This crazy dating world can force you to have to detox from all the dating drama. The wrong Adam can leave a stench on you that can inhibit your real Adam from identifying you. Trust me, I know. I had to get rid of disbelief that I could be loved, hurt, anger, bitterness, loneliness, depression, and more. I asked God to prepare me to be found and seen by my man. I needed a cleansing like the virgins in this text. But once presented, I also needed my Adam to be sure and not double-minded. I have had those claim me, too, because of the wrong motives. They flip-flopped when I did not conform to their body. One day they wanted me, the next they were confused because they could not control me. So, I left them in their confusion and left their stench there, too.

Many men today are unstable in their thoughts with women. They are sleeping for sure because they want to have an entourage or rotate women to their liking. People, I am even talking about church men, too! Sometimes, they can be the worse because they are supposed to know the Lord. God cleanses you and makes you whole, but your Adam still needs to be tweaked. God is still working on him in his slumber so he can one day recognize you and appreciate you for who you really are, not needing a haram. But in the meantime, you make sure you are prepared. God knows the right timing because you deserve God's best. You did not wait all these years to have a dethroned king.

So, prepare yourself and pray for that man indeed to come to you right and whole. Let him, when he finally gets it together, smell a woman that has the smell of God on her. A woman who seems as if she is a virgin though forty. Your very appearance should radiate you are a prize for him sent from God. Get rid of all those unproductive thoughts from your last failed relationship so you can start new. Let your Adam see that you are free from emotional baggage because you have been healed by God! Stay ready, ladies, so when he wakes up, he sees and finds you. I am always trying to better myself with or without him. I know the day will come when we will meet, and I want him to sniff and see the glory of God on me.

Chapter Twenty

DO YOU KNOW WHO YOU ARE?

Ladies, let me tell you something, you are the apple of God's eyes. You were wonderfully and fearfully made by God. Think about it. God let you be the birther and carry life. He let Mary carry the savior for the world. Now that is a lot of love. But somewhere in life, you ran across some man that is not your Adam, and he does not understand your spiritual make up. He can't comprehend with the love of God who you really are. So, he minimizes you, he does not appreciate or cherish you. He plays games with your mind, and you begin to question who you are. You change to fit his program. This Adam seems like he came to destroy the beautiful creature God made you to be. He is not crazy; he just has scales on his eyes that needs to be removed. He is still in a coma and needs some fixing. But you have to be secure in who you are. You have to proclaim the greatness over your life despite your horrible relationships. You have to believe you are loveable and worth it. Many women forget this over time as the years pass, and they are waiting on their Adam.

Case in point. Have you ever seen a woman who just seems to have it going on but something is missing? I am not just talking about her Adam. I am talking about her value in who she is. She is at the top of her game but still doubts she can ever be with a man that really values her. She has been so burnt out that she becomes bitter and just says I can do without a man when she really wants one. Her bad relationships started defining who she is when God created her to be loving, open, caring, soft, and her Adam's helpmate. But she has conditioned herself that she is good and does not realize she has cut herself off because she forgot how wonderful she really is. Women, you must know who you are and be willing to open up again. Yes, your existence is not based on being with a man, but God created us to have a man and to procreate. Procreation is not only with a baby. It means to produce. Period.

I know that two can do more than one. Though we may be fabulous, when we forget that and the Adam shows up, he can't see who we really are. He may show up, and our attitude is so seared we come across like we don't need him. We forgot we were created for him, and we still have an identity. So, we walk around in hurt and unforgiveness of all men which is not from God. Sure, we must protect ourselves and be wise, but we must stay that beautiful loving honest woman God created. Our past relationships should never redefine who we are.

Being defensive does not mean you are sure in who God created you to be. It wears on you even if you have it going on. This attitude can come from being stripped of your identity, so you go into survival mode. Trust me, I get it. I have done it before. I had to cry out to God and say

"Lord, I know you made me to be lovable and caring." I asked God to keep my identity intact so that my disposition does not become jaded when my man is looking for me. I had been so disfigured from bad relationships that God had to put me back together so I could love again. He told me, "Veryl, I did not make you a cold uncaring woman. The world did. You lost who I spoke into existence, so now I have to bring you back around." I had created and became another woman from my hurt, yet I wanted to be married. So, God had to work on my persona that had been ripped from me to be found. He purged me, cleansed me, and opened up my mind to love again. My attitude stunk because the wrong Adams did not speak life over me but wanted me to be who they wanted me to be. They were not concerned with whom God made me to be, so I had to give my perception of me back over to God so he could massage my heart for my right Adam.

The man God sends will not change your spiritual identity or natural beauty from God's master hands of creation.

Chapter Twenty-One

GET YOUR DIGNITY BACK!

Listen, I don't care how low to the floor you went. That last relationship could have drained you of all your peace. But I am here to tell you, I know a God that will pick you up and make you better then you were before. He will heal your wombs from all the lies and disappointments. Get back on track! There is somebody who wants all of you. The good and the bad. There is somebody who will love you the way Christ told man to love his wife. There is a man who does not have scales on his eyes who will see the beauty in you. But by all means don't give up and lose who you are. You were fearfully and wonderfully made by God. Ask him to severe any ties to the no-good man who did not value you. He will break that false covenant relationship up. Don't ponder on him too much. You don't need to go to a dark place of hurt where he was tripping. Let him kick rocks and you do you! There is some man that is going to sniff you and know that your aroma is his aroma. You won't be foreign to him, and he won't try to change you because you are already of his liking.

Get rid of those old pictures that tie you to all those emotions. Let it go! I had to tell myself that. I had to detox like Esther in the Bible so I have a pure scent on me. I don't want no other man's scent on me where I am undetectable. Also, don't bring that other man's drama into your new situation. Now, I am not saying don't be alert or cautious, but when God sends the right one, you can be more apparent. He won't try to scrape you to the coals. But give him a chance. Don't be so hurt you can't even love anymore. I told myself a lie and said I don't need no man! Well, I want one, so I was lying to myself trying to survive. I need my husband. That is the piece I was pulled from. Like I said, there is more greatness with two working together versus one.

Pray, pray, pray for discernment. It is some slick talking men out here even over fifty. The old men play the same games as the younger ones, thinking they are all of that. Where did they learn this from? They are supposed to be the examples, but they act like the young boys.

Don't be naïve like me thinking because someone called you pretty or pretended to have your best interest they meant you well. Naw, even though I am well over fifty they want to get in the panties, too. It's just more disgusting because you would think some of these older men would have more tact. By all means, be your best! Ask God to clean you up and let you soar. Be on top of your game, having stuff together. You have to make it such that the evidence of God's grace on your life is desirable. Look like greatness, smell like greatness, think like greatness, and walk in it! Pick yourself up from those years you lost in a bad relationship. You still have value!

Ask God to show you who you are. What beautiful attributes did he give you? Enhance those and be the crème de la crème. Never ever put yourself down or let anyone else disrespect who you are. Don't change your DNA from God. Be yourself and authentic.

You do not want to pretend to get that man. He wants the real you. You would have to live a lie to make him happy because it was all a show. Be candid that you are not here for games and transparency. By all means, don't date longer than you supposed to with a particular man that you know does not line up with your purpose. Don't waste time. You and your time is valuable. Be soft and let that man know you are here for the real deal, and you will not waste your nor his time. Definitely tap into God for the wisdom in how to deal with this new relationship. I know I have messed up in the past because I said something contrary to what I should have said because I had baggage. Stay positive and don't run the man away that God sends. Be sensitive and listen to God while dating.

Now if you say, I don't know God or I can't hear God, I would admonish you to get to know him! We live in such a self-centered evil world that even church folks play those games. People just don't handle folks with compassion like they used to. Everyone in it for their own elevation. You have to really rely on God for this one, especially if you have so many hits or misses because of your judgment. At this age, I have to hear him. Even my friends have steered me wrong to date men that they had no clue tried to treat me like trash. So, with that being said, throw the old trash out. You need nothing affecting your mentality to love again. Let him go so you can be prosperous in love. You deserve it, and the past hurt can dictate future trauma. Give it to God and move on!

Your man may be sleeping like mine. So now you have to pray and ask God to wake him up! Pray that man out of that coma. Sometimes, men themselves have been through so much, they sleep on the good women. They slide right on past us. Well, today, I am here to ask God with you for you and me. Lord, please snap our men out of their comas and let them see us and claim us. In Jesus Christ's name, we pray AMEN!

THE END BUT MY NEW BEGINNING

About the Author

APOSTLE DR. VERYL HOWARD

Apostle Dr. Veryl Howard, founder of *God's Women in Music, Ministry, Business & Entertainment* tour, *Women Warriors on the Frontline* tour, the *Global Warrior Radio Show*, and Faith Management & Talent Casting, is no stranger to the entertainment world. She has worked with several Gospel greats, such as Deitrick Haddon, Todd Dulaney, Titus Showers, Jekalyn Carr, Lucinda Moore, Pastor Wess Morgan, JJ Hairston, and Caribbean artists DJ Nicholas, Last Call to name a few. She is also a prayer warrior who founded Matthew 6:33 Global Ministries and believes in the power of prayer.

Recently, Dr. Veryl stepped back in the movie business as an actress, producer, and casting director due to it being part of her spiritual assignment. She is also the author of several bestselling books, her most recent being *A General Becomes a Legend*. Her first and second books were *God Hears a Teacher's Cry* and *God Is My Ticket Out the Ghetto*, and she has been published in several other books, to include *Girl, Get Up and Win*, *Prayer Can Change Everything*, and *Beating the Odds*. Her late mom Dr. Virginia Howard, who was the author of *Beating the Odds*, told her she saw her writing gift at the age of five. Her mom edited her initial books up until she was unable to do so due to a stroke. Therefore, Dr. Veryl's zeal to write has become her passion. "This is for mom," she states.

She has been affiliated with several magazines who have featured her or allowed her to be an article writer: *Courageous Woman, She Exist, Mogul, NSPIRE, Totally Lovin Me, I Ascend, Victorious by Design, Devine Glory,* and *Sheen* are just a few. She has also served as a radio and TV host, but most importantly, she views herself as a servant of God, which is why she founded Matthew 6:33 Global Ministries. She believes the ministry gift has opened up the realms of writing by impacting her revelations on matters. This gift has allowed her to be one of Christ's ambassadors who travels the globe to share the Gospel. This enlightened her writing tremendously. Her visits to do ministry work in many third-world countries opened up her eyes to worldwide problems. So, she jots down as God touches her mind and heart while helping others. Her trips to Africa and most of the Caribbean including Antigua, Aruba, Nevis, St. Kitts. St. Marten, Tortola, Guyana, Trinidad, Tobago, St. Lucia, Bahamas, Barbados, Grenada, Petite Martinique, Martinique, Puerto Rico, St. Vincent,

Turks & Caicos, and the Grenadines are just some of the places that helped shape her writing abilities. She is grateful to God for all the downloads while working in ministry in these countries. She feels she is assigned to pray for these countries, and the writing downloads were her blessings from God in her obedience.

"Writing is a must in my life. I am always dreaming up new scripts, books, or sayings," states Apostle Dr. Veryl Howard. As a film/TV producer, eventually, she will take her writing to the screen on another level. But for now, you can find her acting on channels and apps such as BET, Amazon, Tubi, All Black, AMC, and STARZ. She was even a part of a series that was number one for five years called *Double Cross*, where she was the casting director. But for now, she awaits her next movie and has jumped back into the film business and writing her long overdue books.

So, stay tuned to hear what God is doing through her next assignment as a Global Peace Ambassador to the UN consisting on one hundred and ninety-three countries. She said God told her over twenty years ago she would be an ambassador, and she thought, *How?* She attributes this new found success to work in other countries to God's way of expanding her ministry territory to serve. Her passion is to help hurting women, the youth, poverty-stricken families, and senior citizens. She was the care giver for her mom for years and seniors are a priority to her. So, keep this Proverbs 31 woman in prayer as she follows the unction of God for her life. She will continue to be the ambassador for Christ to the nations as God ordained her!

Though Apostle Howard may not exhibit the "bling, bling" with her name in big lights, she believes her "bling, bling" is God.

For booking Dr. Veryl, call Faith Management at 910-644-1824 or email VeryL920@aol.com.

Facebook, Tik Tok and Instagram all are apostleverylhoward.

www.verylhowardministries.net

Dr. Veryl Howard & Family, Her Love

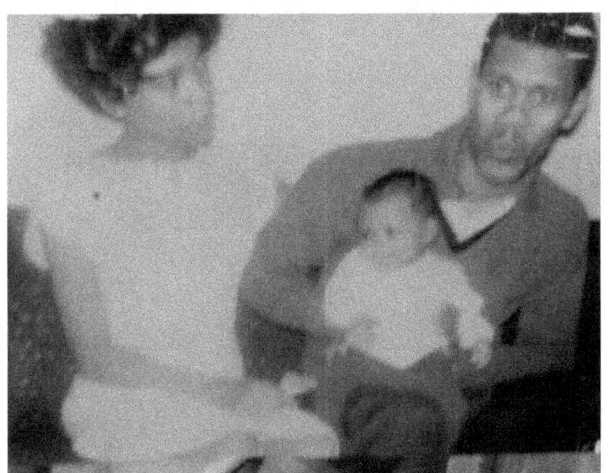

Dr. Veryl as a baby with her mom and dad

Dr. Veryl as a child with her mom

Dr. Veryl, the ballerina

Dr. Veryl and her mom and brothers

Dr. Veryl, the model

Dr. Veryl and her sisters-in-law, Kim & Cynthia

Cowgirl Dr. Veryl

Dr. Veryl and her nieces and nephew

Dr. Veryl's nephews

Dr. Veryl, Plus Size Fashion Week, Milan!

Tickling the ivories

Pretty in Silver

Dr. Veryl Praying!

www.ingramcontent.com/pod-product-compliance
Lightning Source LLC
Chambersburg PA
CBHW071225160426
43196CB00012B/2419